Word 365
Text Formatting

EASY WORD 365 ESSENTIALS - BOOK 1

M.L. HUMPHREY

CONTENTS

Introduction

This book is part of the *Easy Word 365 Essentials* series of titles. These are targeted titles that are excerpted from the main *Word 365 Essentials* series and are focused on one specific topic.

If you want a more general introduction to Word, then you should check out the *Word 365 Essentials* titles instead. In this case, *Word 365 for Beginner*s which covers text formatting in Word as well as other introductory topics.

But if all you want to learn is how to format text in Word, then this is the book for you.

Text Formatting

Text and paragraph formatting is key to working in Word. I have yet to work for an employer who wanted their staff to use Calibri as the font on documents. And I don't think I've ever written a book that didn't use italics or bold. So this chapter is a very important one to master if you're going to use Word.

The text formatting options can be accessed in a number of ways.

First, there are control shortcuts for some of the most basic formatting like Bold (Ctrl + B), Italics (Ctrl + I), and Underline (Ctrl + U).

Second, in the Font section of the Home tab you can find the most common formatting choices:

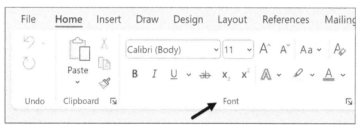

Third, the expansion arrow there as well as right-clicking and choosing Font from the dropdown menu in your document will both open the Font dialogue box. This can also be opened by using Ctrl + D.

Finally, there is a mini formatting menu that you can see if you right-click in your document:

For each of the above options, first select the text you want to format, and then apply the formatting option using the method you prefer.

Let's now walk through what your formatting options are. I'm going to do this alphabetically so you can easily return to this chapter when needed, although you can also use the index in the back of the print version of this book or search in the ebook.

Bold

To bold text I usually just use Ctrl + B.

The Font dialogue box allows you to choose either Bold or Bold Italic.

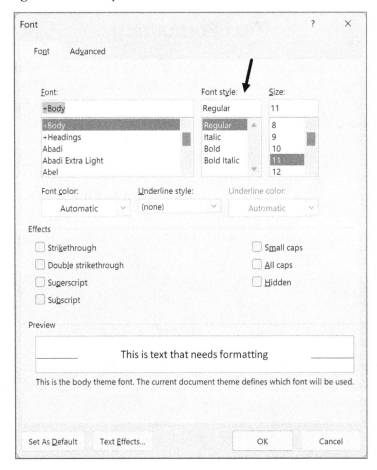

You can also click on the capital B on the left-hand side of the Font section of the Home tab or the mini formatting menu.

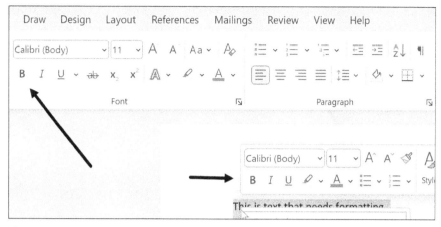

To remove bolding from text, you can either use Ctrl + B again, click on the capital B once more, or in the Font dialogue box change the Font Style to Regular or Italic.

For the first three options, if the text you selected was partially bolded and partially not, the first time you select the option it will bold all of the text, so you will need to do it twice to remove the bolding. (That usually happens to me if I select a range of text and there's a space at the end that wasn't formatted as bold that I can't tell isn't formatted the same way.)

Change Case

It is possible to change your selected text so that all of the letters are in uppercase, lowercase, sentence case (where the first letter of each sentence is upper case but the rest is lower case), toggle case (where the first letter of each word is lower case and the rest are in upper case), or where each word is capitalized but the rest of the letters are lower case.

I do this through the Font section of the Home tab using the Change Case option in the top row on the right-hand side. It's represented by an Aa where there is a capital letter A next to a lower-case one.

Here you can see the dropdown choices as well as examples of each one in the document:

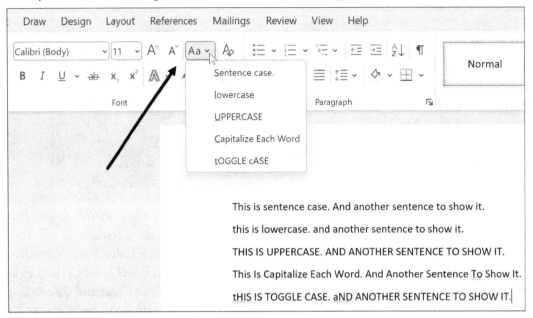

Change case is also an option in the mini formatting menu.

The Font dialogue box also has checkboxes for Small Caps and All Caps.

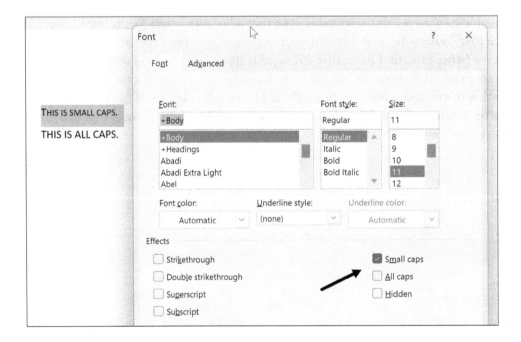

Font Color

Font color is another one that I usually apply using the Font section of the Home tab. It's the A with a red line under it, at least by default. (Once you change the color that new color will be the color under the A.) It is also available in the mini formatting menu as well as in the Font Color dropdown menu of the Font dialogue box.

In the Home tab, if you just want the color shown under the A (which is red by default), click on the A. Otherwise, click on the dropdown arrow to see seventy different font colors you can choose from:

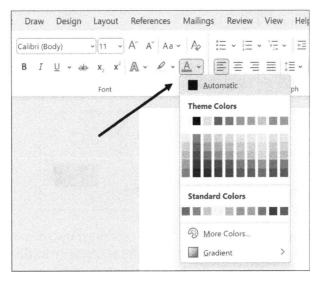

If one of those seventy colors isn't what you want or you have a specific color that you're required to use, click on More Colors to bring up the Colors dialogue box.

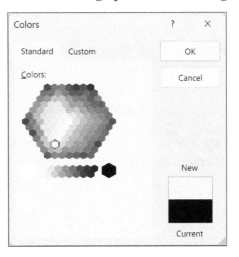

The first tab of that dialogue box is labeled Standard and shows a honeycomb of colors. Click on any of those colors in the honeycomb or in the white-to-gray-to-black line below that to choose a color. The new color will show at the top of the square in the bottom right corner of the dialogue box. The old color will show on the bottom of that square.

Click OK to apply the new color or use the X in the top right corner to close the dialogue box without applying a new color.

If you need to use a custom color, click over to the Custom tab.

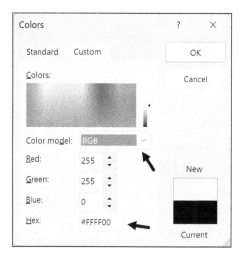

It has a rainbow color grid that you can click into and then use the slider on the side to adjust the degree of black included in the color. But the real power in this tab is below that. The dropdown lets you choose between RGB or HSL colors and there is also a Hex Code box at the very bottom.

If you have a custom color you must use, which many corporations do, you can get the exact color you need by providing the RGB, HSL, or Hex Code value on this tab. Once you've done so, click OK to apply it to your selected text.

The mini formatting menu and Font dialogue box work the exact same way. They both have a dropdown menu of colors to choose from.

Font Size

If you ever need to change the size of your text, there are a number of options available. The one I use is the dropdown menu in the top row of the Font section of the Home tab:

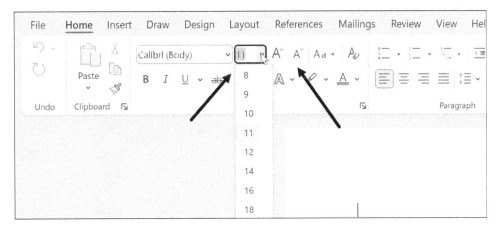

Click on the dropdown arrow and choose the font size you want from there. The default in Word is 11 pt, so a number less than that will be smaller text and a number greater than that will be larger. If you're not sure what size you want, you can hold your mouse over the different values and the text will change size within your document. To keep that change, click on the value.

You can also click into that box and type a value if you want. As you can see in the dropdown, it only includes the most popular sizes, so if you want something like 13 pt text you need to manually enter that value.

Another option is located to the right of that dropdown. There are two A's there, one with an up arrow, one with a down arrow. Clicking on those options will move the font size up or down one size. The font sizes used for that are the same as the ones in the dropdown. So you would move from 12 pt to 14 pt to 16 pt, for example.

The mini formatting menu also has those same options available. And the Font dialogue box has a list of popular font sizes to choose from as well as a box where you can type in a value.

Font Type

To the left of the font size dropdown is the Font dropdown. This is available in the Font section of the Home tab, in the mini formatting menu, and also in the Font dialogue box.

Here is the font dropdown from the Home tab:

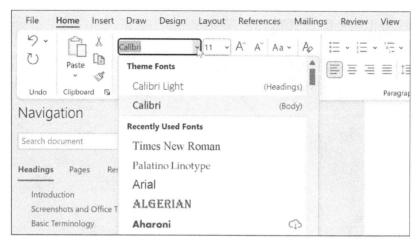

The default font in Word is Calibri. If you use a different Theme in Word you may have a different default. Those Theme Fonts will be listed first. Next you will see Recently Used Fonts listed. And then finally you will see an alphabetical listing of all available fonts.

Which fonts are listed will depend on your computer. Word comes with a number of default fonts, but it is possible to buy additional fonts as well. I have a number of those so my font listing may be different from yours.

If you know the font you want, you can click into the box with the current font name in it and start typing the font name like I've done here:

I typed "Gara" and Word took me to that portion of my fonts list and also suggested the

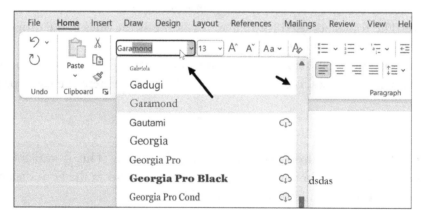

Garamond font which is the only one that starts with those letters.

There are also scroll bars available on the right-hand side of the font listing that you can use to scroll through your listed fonts.

Each font is written using that font so you can see what it looks like. That's why, for example, Georgia Pro Black is so dark compared to the rest, because a black-weight font is a very bold weight. You can also see there the difference between Gautami, which is a non-serif font, and Georgia, which is a serifed font.

Usually, in a corporate or school environment you will be told which font or fonts to use. For example, with writing, Times New Roman is a common one to use. In the past Courier was a common one. One employer I worked for preferred Palatino for everything.

If no one gives you guidance on which font to use, keep in mind your goal or purpose. In general, that is going to be legibility. You want people to be able to read the words you write.

For a standard audience reading a book like this one, that means using a serifed font, like Times New Roman or Palatino. Serifed fonts have little feet at the bottom of the letters which are supposed to make it easier to read words.

For those who have difficulty with sight, so large-print readers for example, often a non-serifed font is a better choice. For my large print fiction titles, for example, I use Verdana.

Save the display fonts (like Algerian) and script fonts (like Cochocib) for signage or book covers or report covers. And even then, be careful to make sure that people can actually read the text.

Now, there is a new quirk in Word 365 that we should also discuss and that's those little cloud download options in that font listing. Those are fonts that are available to you to use through Word, but that are not installed on your computer. To use one of those fonts, you'd need to click on that cloud to download the font.

It is possible to disable this if they annoy you and you don't want them. To do so, go to File and then click on Account at the bottom left corner of the screen. From the Account page click on Manage Settings under Account Privacy. That will open a Privacy Settings dialogue box. You can then uncheck the box for Experiences That Download Online Content.

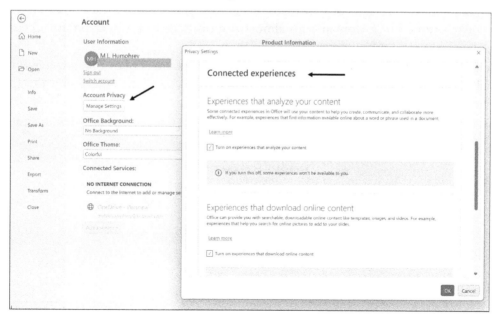

When you restart Word, you should no longer have those downloadable fonts listed. Much cleaner:

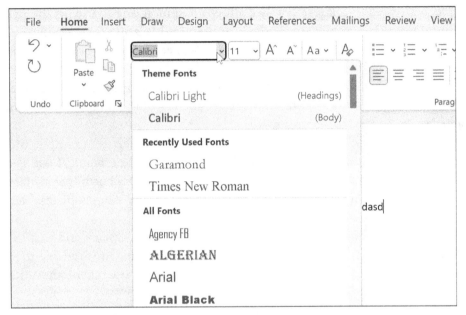

(And I should note here that I actually scrolled a little below that and unchecked the box for everything. But now I have to go and check it again so I can keep writing this book for you. There are quirks in Word 365 that are driven by those settings or by being online. For example, I learned that the Read Aloud voice in Word 365 is the old mechanical male-sounding horrible one if you're offline but a woman who almost sounds decent if you're online. Technology. Always changing.)

One more thing to mention here is that different fonts, even ones that are the same font size, will appear different sizes on the page. So choose your font before you do any final formatting or arrangement of elements.

Here are a few examples of good, solid, reliable fonts you can use that also demonstrates that:

Each of the fonts in the list above are the same font pt size.

Highlight Text

If you ever want to highlight text, like you would physically with a highlighter, you can do that using the Text Highlight Color option. By default it's going to have a bright yellow line under what looks like a marker. It's located in the bottom row of the Font section of the Home tab next to font color.

Select your text and then if all you want is yellow highlight, click on that image.

If you want to choose a different color, like I did here with a bright green, use the dropdown arrow:

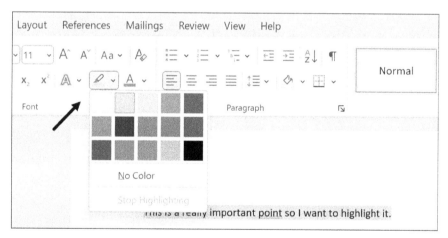

To remove a highlight, use the No Color option.

The highlight color option is also available in the mini formatting menu.

Do not confuse this with adding fill color to a cell in a table. Also, it's better to use track changes and comments to flag any issues in a document rather than use the highlighter for that purpose. Track changes, comments, and tables are intermediate-level topics covered in the next book in this series, but I just wanted to mention it here in case.

Italicize

To italicize text, the easiest way is to use Ctrl + I. But the Font section of the Home tab and the mini formatting menu also have a slanted I that you can click on in the bottom row under the font dropdown. And the Font dialogue box has options for both Italic and Bold Italic under font style.

To remove italics, select your text and then once more use Ctrl + I or click on the slanted I in the Font section of the Home tab or in the mini formatting menu. You can also change the font style back to Regular or to Bold in the Font dialogue box. As with bolding, if you select text that is partially italicized you will need to use Ctrl + I or click on the slanted I twice because the first time will apply it to all of the text and the second will remove it.

Strikethrough

To add a basic strikethrough to text, you can use the ab with a strikethrough in the Font section of the Home tab or the mini formatting menu. In the mini formatting menu it's off to the right side:

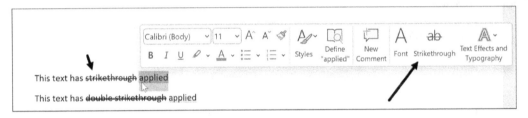

Above you can see an example of what that looks like when applied to the word "strikethrough" in the first line of text.

If you want a double strikethrough, like in the second line of text, then you need to use the Font dialogue box. There is a checkbox there for double strikethrough.

Subscript or Superscript

To apply subscript or superscript to text, use the options in the Font section of the Home tab.

Subscript looks like an X with a 2 in the subscript position. Superscript looks like an X with a 2 in the superscript position.

You can see examples of text using them in the screenshot on the next page.

Simply select the text that needs that formatting and then click on the option. So in the examples shown below, I selected the 2 in each line of text and then applied the appropriate formatting to it.

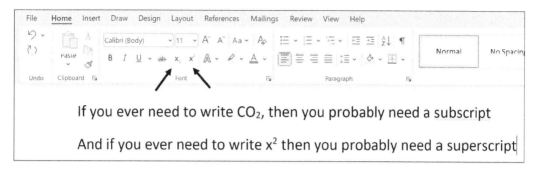

Subscript and superscript are also available as checkboxes in the Font dialogue box.

Text Effects

I'm only mentioning text effects here because they're included in the Font section of the Home tab. For new users to Word you are very unlikely to need these. But what they do is let you add an outline, shadow, reflection, glow, or other effect to your text. If you click on the dropdown arrow for Text Effects you'll see a number of pre-formatted options as well.

All I'll say here about these is that you should keep in mind your audience and effectively using text to convey your message. It is far too easy to add outlines and shadows and glow and reflections to text and end up overwhelming the text itself. So proceed with caution.

Underline

The easiest way to underline text is to use Ctrl + U. That will add a single-line underline below your selected text. You can also click on the underlined U in the Font section of the Home tab or in the mini formatting menu.

Unlike bold and italics, there is more than one underline option you can apply. To see a short list of choices, click on the dropdown arrow next to the underlined U in the Font section of the Home tab to see a list of your available choices:

There is a single line, double line, thick line, dotted line, dashed line, two lines that have both dots and dashes, as well as a wavy line.

As you hold your mouse over each option, Word will apply it to your text so you can see what it will look like. Click on the one you want.

You can also choose a color for your underline at the bottom of that dropdown.

Clicking on More Underlines will open the Font dialogue box which has an Underline Style dropdown menu with even more choices available. Select the underline style you want there and then click OK to apply it.

The Words Only option will place a single underline under each of the selected words, but not carry through that underline between the words. Like so:

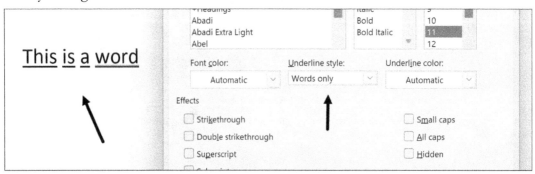

To remove an underline, use Ctrl + U or click on the underlined U once more. If you used an underline other than the default single-line option, you will have to do so twice because the first time will convert the existing underline to a single-line underline.

Another option for removing an underline is to use the dropdown for underline in the Font section of the Home tab and click on the None option towards the bottom.

The Font dialogue box also has a (none) option you can select.

$$* * *$$

Clear All Formatting

We just covered all of the formatting options in the Font section of the Home tab, but there's one more option in the top right corner there:

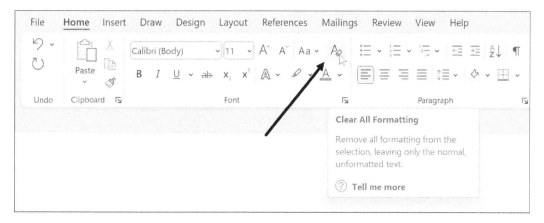

This is the Clear All Formatting option. Click on that to remove all formatting from your selected text. Below you can see text in the first row that has a change in font and font size as well as bold, italics, underline, strikethrough, text effects, highlight, and a red color applied.

This is a sentence *that* I want to test

This is a sentence that I want to test

In the second row is that same text after I used Clear All Formatting. It changed the font and font size back to the default of Calibri 11 pt and removed all other formatting except for the highlight.

Format Painter

The Format Painter is possibly my favorite tool in Microsoft Word. I cannot tell you how many projects I have worked on where there has been some weird slight difference between paragraphs written by different team members. No one ever knows how the change got in there and no one can figure out how to fix it.

The answer is to use the Format Painter tool. It is located in the Clipboard section of the Home tab and also available in the mini formatting menu:

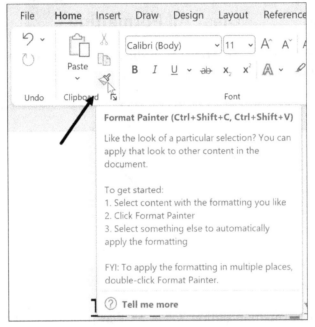

I always think of it as the format sweeper because it looks like a broom to me, but it's official name is the Format Painter.

What it does is takes the formatting of your selected text and places that formatting on other text that you select.

So step one is to select the text that has the formatting you want.

Step two is to click on the Format Painter. Double-click if you have more than one location where you want to transfer the formatting.

Step three is to select the text where you want to apply your formatting. Use the mouse or the trackpad to select the text. (Using the Shift and arrow keys doesn't work.)

If you have text that you select that has a wide variety of formatting, like in our example above for clear formatting, Word will generally go with the formatting that is at the beginning of the selection. So in that case it would transfer the bold and underline from "this" but not all the rest of the formatting.

Where Format Painter really shines in my opinion is when it's used to transfer paragraph formatting which can include the space before and after the paragraph, the space between lines in the paragraph, any indent that paragraph may have, etc. It will capture all of that.

And I don't know if this is still the case, but it's something to be aware of. Sometimes in the past it would matter whether I selected a paragraph from the first word to the last instead of from the last word to the first. So if I transferred formatting using the Format Painter and it didn't seem to fix the issue the first time, I'd go back and select the paragraph starting at the opposite end and try it again.

This can be especially true with numbered or bulleted lists.

Another trick to try is to select more than one paragraph if spacing between paragraphs matters.

Also, formatting can be transferred from one document to another. It doesn't have to be done within the same document.

When you transfer formatting this way, all of the existing formatting in the paragraph you're transferring to will be removed. It's all or nothing. (That includes italics, for example, so if you have italics in text in your document and you use the Format Painter you will lose that word-level formatting.)

If you double-click on the Format Painter so you can use it in more than one location, use Esc or click on it once more in the menu bar to turn it off when you're done.

Appendix A: Basic Terminology Recap

These terms were covered in detail in *Word 365 for Beginners*. This is just meant as a refresher.

Tab

When I refer to a tab, I am referring to the menu options at the top of the screen. The tab options that are available by default are File, Home, Insert, Draw, Design, Layout, References, Mailings, Review, View, and Help, but for certain tasks additional tabs will appear.

Click

If I tell you to click on something, that means to move your cursor over to that location and then either right-click or left-click. If I don't say which to do, left-click.

Left-Click / Right-Click

A left-click is generally for selecting something and involves using the left-hand side of your mouse or bottom left-hand corner of your trackpad. A right-click is generally for opening a dropdown menu and involves using the right-hand side of your mouse or bottom right-hand corner of your trackpad.

Left-Click and Drag

Left-click and drag means to left-click and then hold that left-click as you move your mouse.

Dropdown Menu

A dropdown menu is a list of choices that you can view by right-clicking in a specific spot or clicking on an arrow next to or below one of the available choices under the tabs up top. Depending on where you are in the workspace, a dropdown menu may actually drop upward from that spot.

Expansion Arrow

In the bottom right corner of some of the sections under the tabs in the top menu you will see an arrow, which I refer to as an expansion arrow. Clicking on an expansion arrow will usually open a dialogue box or task pane and is often the way to see the largest number of options.

Dialogue Box

A dialogue box is a pop-up box that will open on top of your workspace and will usually include the largest number of choices for that particular setting or task.

Scroll Bar

Scroll bars appear when there are more options than can appear on the screen or when your document is longer than will show on the screen. They can be used to move through the remainder of the choices or document.

Task Pane

A task pane is a set of additional options that will appear to the sides or even below the main workspace. The Navigation pane is by default visible on the left-hand side of the workspace. You can close a task pane by clicking on the X in the top right corner of the pane.

Control Shortcuts

Control shortcuts are shortcuts that let you perform certain tasks in Word. I will write them as Ctrl + and then a character. That means to hold down both the Ctrl key and that character. So Ctrl + C means hold down Ctrl and C, which will let you copy your selection. Even though I will write each shortcut using a capital letter it doesn't have to be the capitalized version to work.

About the Author

M.L. Humphrey is a former stockbroker with a degree in Economics from Stanford and an MBA from Wharton who has spent close to twenty years as a regulator and consultant in the financial services industry.

You can reach M.L. at mlhumphreywriter@gmail.com or at mlhumphrey.com.

www.ingramcontent.com/pod-product-compliance
Lightning Source LLC
Chambersburg PA
CBHW082106070326
40689CB00054B/4744